21st Century Skills INNOVATION *Library*

From Kingfishers to . . . Bullet Trains

by Wil Mara

CHERRY LAKE
Publishing

Published in the United States of America by Cherry Lake Publishing
Ann Arbor, Michigan
www.cherrylakepublishing.com

Content Adviser: Mariappan Jawaharlal, PhD, Professor of Mechanical Engineering, California State
Polytechnic University, Pomona, California

Design: The Design Lab

Photo Credits: Cover (main) and page 1, ©Hxdbzxy/Dreamstime.com; cover (inset) and page 18,
©Mircea BEZERGHEANU/Shutterstock, Inc.; page 4, ©Darren Hedges/Shutterstock, Inc.; page 6,
©R Carner/Shutterstock, Inc.; page 7, ©iStockphoto.com/mura; page 9, ©Tristan Scholze/
Shutterstock, Inc.; page 10, ©Stefan1992/Dreamstime.com; pages 13, 23, and 27, ©Thomas
Nord/Shutterstock.com; page 14, ©Dennis Donohue/Shutterstock, Inc.; page 16, ©iStockphoto.
com/peart; page 17, ©Karel Gallas/Shutterstock, Inc.; page 20, ©SeanPavonePhoto/
Shutterstock.com; page 21, ©egd/Shutterstock, Inc.; page 25, ©World History Archive/
Alamy; page 28, ©Everett Collection Inc/Alamy.

Library of Congress Cataloging-in-Publication Data
Mara, Wil.
 From kingfishers to . . . bullet trains/by Wil Mara.
     p. cm.–(Nature's inventors) (Innovation library)
 Includes bibliographical references and index.
 ISBN 978-1-61080-498-1 (lib. bdg.) — ISBN 978-1-61080-585-8 (e-book) —
 ISBN 978-1-61080-672-5 (pbk.)
 1. High speed trains–Juvenile literature. 2. Birds–Flight–Juvenile literature. I. Title.
 TF1455.M37 2012
 625.2'3–dc23   2012005747

Cherry Lake Publishing would like to acknowledge
the work of The Partnership for 21st Century Skills.
Please visit www.21stcenturyskills.org *for more information.*

Printed in the United States of America
Corporate Graphics Inc.
July 2012
CLFA11

CONTENTS

CHAPTER ONE

Speeding Through History

Steam locomotives are still used in some places.

Have you ever watched a train go by? It's pretty fast, isn't it? For centuries, humans have been trying to develop better methods of shipping cargo and people that are both fast and safe. We've been successful so far. But continuing to unlock the secrets of nature is a key to improving things even more.

Railroads, in one form or another, have been around for thousands of years. The earliest type was probably the Diolkos pathways of ancient Greece. They were built and operated during the 6th century BCE. Wagons were pulled along the Diolkos by either people or animals. The wagons' wheels rolled through grooves that the Greeks made in the road. The grooves were not exactly the same as rails, but their purpose was similar. They were made to keep the wagons in place so they wouldn't veer off course.

In the 1500s, wooden rails were used in the European nation of Austria. Surprisingly, the earliest known line in that country is still in use today, although it has been upgraded with modern materials and equipment. Metal rails began to replace wooden ones in the 1700s. The wheels of a vehicle rolled better on a metal surface, and metal lasted longer and required fewer repairs. Around the same time, wheel design began to change. Most importantly, a **flange** was added to the wheel to keep the wheel on the track.

By the start of the 19th century, the first steam-powered locomotive had been developed, and a steam-powered rail system was operating in England. It was so successful that similar railway networks were built in other parts of Europe. By this time, railroad cars were carrying both cargo and people, who were delighted with the opportunity to travel so quickly to faraway places.

Asia and the Americas began to lay down their own tracks in the mid-1800s, and by the end of the century their systems were well established. Germany was the first nation to power its trains with electricity, in the 1880s. In the early 1900s, electrical power began

Diesel locomotives are used to pull both cargo and passenger trains.

The Shinkansen line changed the way people travel in Japan.

to be used in combination with **diesel** fuel as a way of powering locomotives. By the middle of the 20th century, this technology had become common in many areas.

In 1964, traveling by train entered a new era with the now-famous Shinkansen line in Japan. Its high-speed trains traveled at tremendous speeds, bringing people

to their destinations faster than ever before. The Shinkansen ran between the Japanese capital of Tokyo and one of its busiest industrial centers, the city of Osaka. Today, the Shinkansen's "bullet trains" can reach speeds of 185 mph (300 kilometers per hour). They carry more than 150 million passengers each year, run solely on electricity, and have never had a passenger death because of a crash or derailment. In addition, the trains are environment-friendly, emitting only 15 percent of the carbon dioxide that's released by an automobile on a similar journey.

Other countries have used the ideas behind the Shinkansen to develop their own bullet trains. The popularity of bullet trains shows that they are the future of rail service around the world. But as with any human invention, bullet trains have had their share of problems. And when designers had to solve those problems, they found solutions in the most amazing place.

CHAPTER TWO

Hey, Turn That Down!

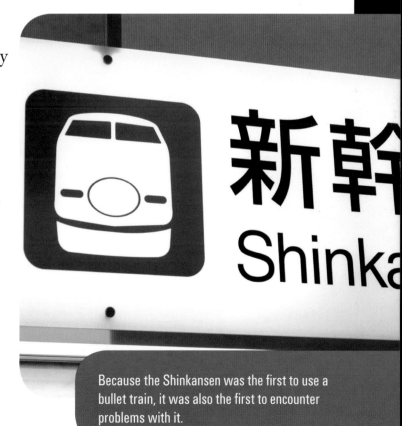

Advances in technology present fascinating possibilities for us to explore. However, they also tend to create frustrating new problems. When this happens, the most inventive minds in the world are called upon to come up with solutions. The bullet train was no different from any other groundbreaking creation.

Two of the most challenging problems

Because the Shinkansen was the first to use a bullet train, it was also the first to encounter problems with it.

Pantographs connect electric trains to power lines.

with Japan's bullet train had to do with the loud noise it produced. The first problem involved the train's **pantograph**. A pantograph is an antenna-like device with rods and wires that sits on the roof of a train car. The device makes contact with the overhead electrical lines that provide the train with its power. Because the train was moving at such blazing speeds, the air blowing over the pantograph produced an unusually high level of noise. The Japanese government had strict regulations on how much noise was allowed. They did not want people close to the railroad to be disturbed in their homes and offices. In the past, noise wasn't as much of a nuisance because ordinary trains weren't reaching the speeds of the bullet train.

The second noise-related problem involved tunnels. Because the line travels across mountainous regions, about half of the Shinkansen's route is through tunnels bored through the mountains. When the bullet train charged into a tunnel, it increased the atmospheric pressure inside the tunnel. The increase in pressure became waves of energy that traveled at the speed of sound, 768 miles per hour (1,236 kph). When the waves were forced out of the tunnel's other side, they created a sonic boom of tremendous force and volume. The waves also caused vibrations in the surrounding

Learning & Innovation Skills

 The Japanese government places a high priority on passenger comfort, so the Shinkansen tracks were laid out without steep rises or drops. Another interesting feature of the bullet trains is that they usually run in areas where there are very few car roadways. This largely eliminates the possibility of accidents caused by cars being driven onto the tracks. Japan also has strict laws forbidding people from driving on or near the rails. People who break these laws are subject to heavy fines and possible imprisonment.

area that rattled homes and other buildings, similar to the tremors of a minor earthquake. The Japanese government ordered the design **engineers** to find a solution. While they were at work seeking answers, the bullet train was forced to run at lower speeds. Unable to quickly come up with a solution, people feared that the train would have to run at lower speeds permanently.

Then along came a team of engineers led by a man named Eiji Nakatsu. But Nakatsu wasn't just an engineer—he was also a bird-watcher.

The Shinkansen routes are planned to avoid heavily populated areas.

CHAPTER THREE

What in the World Is Biomimicry?

Owls inspired Nakatsu to solve the problem of noisy pantographs.

Nakatsu and his team were given the task of trying to solve the bullet train's noise problems. At first, they were stumped and could not find a solution. Then Nakatsu, who had been fascinated by birds all his life, met an aircraft designer named Seiichi Yajima at a meeting of a bird enthusiast's organization. Yajima mentioned that a great deal of aircraft technology had been based on the design of birds' bodies and how birds moved through the air. The practice of using nature as a model to create or improve upon human-made items is known as **biomimicry**. Yajima's comments got Nakatsu thinking. If certain aircraft problems could be solved through biomimicry, why not the noise difficulties with the bullet train?

First, Nakatsu tackled the problem of the noisy pantographs. He hoped to find species of birds that traveled at high speeds while producing very little noise. He found his answer in owls. These nighttime hunters caught their **prey** by swooping down and grabbing it in almost total silence. Nakatsu and his team discovered that owls have tiny, sawtooth-shaped feathers along the edges of their larger wing feathers. Each time the wings flapped, these tiny feathers "broke up" the swirling air before it had a chance to make any noise.

The air produced by the flapping wings of other birds spins into an invisible mass called a **vortex**. But an owl's edge feathers disperse this air into thousands of tinier vortices, making the air much quieter. Nakatsu's team was able to create a similar effect for pantographs by adding strips of wing-shaped metal with notched edges. This greatly reduced the level of noise produced by the train.

The world of birds also offered a solution to the problem of the sonic booms created in tunnels. A bullet train passenger had told Nakatsu that it felt as though the train suddenly "shrank" every time it entered a tunnel. Nakatsu believed the train was experiencing a sudden change in surrounding air pressure, going from a low-**resistance** environment (ordinary air outside the tunnel) to a high-resistance environment (pressurized air

Tunnels are not a problem for regular trains because these trains do not move as fast as bullet trains do.

Nakatsu looked to a small bird called the kingfisher for clues on how to solve one of the bullet train's sound problems.

inside the tunnel). Nakatsu once again looked to nature for answers, this time hoping to find a creature that traveled between low- and high-resistance environments.

Nakatsu focused on the kingfisher, a small, brightly colored bird that included fish in its diet. To catch its

Kingfishers move very fast as they dive down to snatch unsuspecting prey from the water and they make almost no noise as they do so.

prey, the kingfisher has to fly over the water, and then quickly swoop down and break through the water's surface. The tiny bird had to make as little noise—and as little splash—as possible. Nakatsu determined that the kingfisher accomplished this with its long, slender beak. Nakatsu's team redesigned the nose of the bullet train to look like the beak. Their design worked perfectly. Tunnel noise was reduced by more than 25 percent. The train, with its new 50-foot (15-meter) kingfisher-shaped nose, also uses 15 percent less electricity and travels 10 percent faster than it did with its earlier design.

Learning & Innovation Skills

Using properties of bird anatomy to reduce noise problems in the bullet train isn't the only example of biomimicry that humans have used to their advantage. Engineers in Africa studied termite mounds, which maintain steady temperatures and humidity regardless of the environment around them. Developing technology based on their observations, the engineers constructed an office building that remained cool without the aid of air-conditioning. Researchers studying bats, which use high-pitched sounds to guide them through darkness, have used this technology to make products for blind people. In the future, scientists hope to copy the silk made by spiders, which is stronger than steel.

CHAPTER FOUR

The Future of Bullet Trains

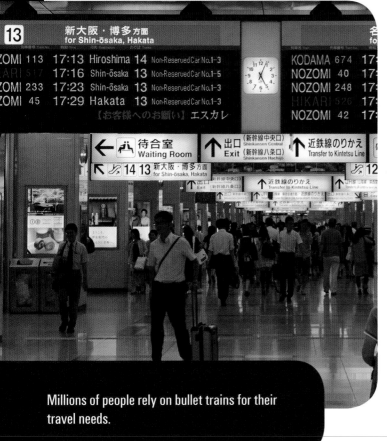

13 新大阪・博多方面
for Shin-ōsaka, Hakata

ZOMI 113 17:13 Hiroshima 14 Non-Reserved Car No.1-3
KARI 517 17:16 Shin-ōsaka 13 Non-Reserved Car No.1-5
ZOMI 233 17:23 Shin-ōsaka 13 Non-Reserved Car No.1-3
ZOMI 45 17:29 Hakata 13 Non-Reserved Car No.1-3
【お客様へのお願い】エスカレ

KODAMA 674 17:
NOZOMI 40 17:
NOZOMI 248 17:
HIKARI 526 17:
NOZOMI 42 17:

← 🚻 待合室 Waiting Room
↑ 出口 （新幹線中央口） Exit （新幹線八条口） Shinkansen Central Shinkansen Hachijō
↑ 近鉄線のりかえ Transfer to Kintetsu Line

14 13 新大阪・博多方面 for Shin-ōsaka, Hakata

Millions of people rely on bullet trains for their travel needs.

Getting people to and from their destinations more quickly results in a huge savings of time. The Japanese government has estimated that the time saved on the Shinkansen line has amounted to hundreds of millions of workers' hours. Workers spend more time at their jobs, being productive, and less time sitting on a train waiting to get to work.

The positive effect that bullet trains have on

Bullet trains provide a faster, more environmentally friendly alternative to driving.

the environment is also significant. Diesel fuel, which pollutes the environment, is not being used. More people are choosing to ride the bullet trains than drive their automobiles. This results in fewer traffic jams and a

considerable reduction of carbon dioxide being emitted into the air.

Although the redesign of the bullet train's nose and pantographs have reduced noise levels, engineers have had to erect expensive sound barriers in some areas. Fallen snow has also presented difficulties. In areas where snowfall is particularly heavy, bullet trains have to travel more slowly. Sprinklers have been added around the tracks in an attempt to melt the snow before it piles up too high, but this has only been moderately successful.

Also, bullet trains cost a great deal of money to build. A few nations are still paying for bullet trains that they have already built. In some cases, bullet trains are so expensive that private companies have to help their governments pay for the costs.

Meanwhile, designers are hard at work to solve problems caused by wind resistance. They believe that bullet trains could go faster if there was a way to reduce

Bullet trains represent the future of train travel around the world. There is a good chance *you* may be riding on one someday soon.

the amount of wind blowing into the gap between each train car. It has been suggested that some type of "skin" could be used, one that would wrap over the gaps and stretch when the train travels around curves at high speed. Increasing the speed of bullet trains, however, still appears to be the main goal for engineering teams worldwide. Although trains that top 250 miles per hour (400 kph) have operated, the "need for speed" must be balanced with concerns over safety, noise, construction costs, and the price of a passenger's ticket.

Bullet trains are here to stay. The answers to all their future problems might just be waiting to be discovered in the wild world of plants and animals.

CHAPTER FIVE

The All-Star Team

Many notable figures have contributed to the development of trains through the years. Here are a few who have left their marks on the tracks.

Richard Trevithick (1771–1833) was one of the fathers of steam-powered travel. Born in Great Britain, he spent much of his early life in the mining business. He became a mine engineer in 1797,

Richard Trevithick made important advances in steam engine technology.

Life & Career Skills

Engineering is a fascinating scientific field and one worth considering as a career choice. An engineer is a problem solver who uses his or her knowledge in many different areas—including aerospace, mining, computers, electronics, agriculture, architecture, and other fields. Engineers are required to exercise a high degree of creativity and innovative thinking. Engineers are often highly paid. If you choose a career in engineering, you'll most likely be challenged to push your talents to their limit, and you will have the chance to make the world a better place through your hard work.

during which time he worked on improving engines that ran on the power of steam pressure. In 1801, he built a working steam locomotive, which he called the Puffing Devil. It ran on an ordinary road rather than a set of rails. In 1808, Trevithick built the first model that ran on railroad tracks. He later took on other engineering projects, including improvements in ship design. His steam-powered engine led the way to widespread use of steam locomotives in rail travel.

Hideo Shima (1901–1998) began his engineering career in train development in 1925 when he joined Japan's Ministry of Railways. He improved gear and driving wheel efficiency on steam locomotives in his native country. As head engineer for the Japanese National Railways, his involvement with the Shinkansen bullet train network included designing the track layout, the electrical facilities, and

The Shinkansen line would not be what it is today without the work of Hideo Shima.

the innovative train cars. In 1969, he took over the top position at the National Space Development Agency of Japan, where he led the nation's early space projects.

As one of Japan's most prominent 20th-century engineers, Shima was honored by his government with the prestigious Order of Cultural Merit in 1994.

Henry Bessemer's steel production techniques helped increase construction of railroads and many other products.

Henry Bessemer (1813–1898) took an early interest in metals. In 1850, he began research to produce steel quickly and inexpensively for the purpose of making weapons and ammunition for the military. He eventually came up with the idea of blowing air through raw, molten ore. This technique helped burn out all of the elements that needed to be removed for the ore to become steel. Bessemer's discovery not only helped make weapons, but it was also useful in producing rails for railroad travel. The "Bessemer Process" became the standard for steel production for more than 100 years.

Alejandro Goicoechea (1895–1984), born in Spain, used his skills in engineering to build defenses to help his country during the Spanish Civil War (1936–1939). He oversaw design and construction of a series of walls, trenches, bunkers, and tunnels along the coast and mountains of Bilbao, one of Spain's northern cities. In 1945, he improved diesel-powered trains by altering the design of the axles so that the train's center of gravity shifted from the sides to the middle. In doing so, the train could move around curves at much higher speeds than before. Some of this technology was later adapted to high-speed trains, eliminating the need to slow them down when taking sharp turns.

Glossary

biomimicry (bye-oh-MI-mi-kree) the practice of copying nature to build or improve something

diesel (DEE-zuhl) a fuel used in certain engines that is heavier than gasoline

engineers (en-juh-EERZ) people who are trained to design and build machines, vehicles, or other structures

flange (FLANJ) a rim or edge on a wheel, used to strengthen an object or hold it in place

funicular (fu-NIH-kue-luhr) a railway that is built onto a slope or other grade and operates by a cable system

pantograph (PAN-teh-graf) an antenna-like collection of rods and wires that transmits power from overhead electrical wires to a locomotive

prey (PRAY) an animal that is hunted by another animal for food

resistance (ri-ZISS-tuhnss) a force that opposes the motion of an object

vortex (VOR-teks) a swirling mass of air or water

For More Information

BOOKS

Graham, Ian. *Bullet Trains and Other Fast Machines on Rails*. Irvine, CA: QED Publishing, 2010.

Lee, Dora. *Biomimicry: Inventions Inspired by Nature*. Tonawanda, NY: Kids Can Press, 2011.

McMahon, Peter. *Ultimate Trains*. Tonawanda, NY: Kids Can Press, 2010.

Von Finn, Denny. *Bullet Trains*. Minneapolis: Bellwether Media, 2009.

WEB SITES

Ask Nature: What Is Biomimicry?
www.asknature.org/article/view/what_is_biomimicry
Find out more about biomimicry, with examples, further links, and interesting video content.

Railway Technology: Shinkansen, Japan
www.railway-technology.com/projects/shinkansen
A good overview of the famous Shinkansen railway, with details about its basic technology, how it functions every day, and proposed future developments.

Index

About the Author

Wil Mara is the award-winning author of more than 120 books, many of which are educational titles for young readers. More information about his work can be found at www.wilmara.com.